# The Dime Store Joseph

Kathleen Kilgallon

Published by Kathleen Kilgallon, 2021.

While every precaution has been taken in the preparation of this book, the publisher assumes no responsibility for errors or omissions, or for damages resulting from the use of the information contained herein.

THE DIME STORE JOSEPH

**First edition. November 30, 2021.**

Copyright © 2021 Kathleen Kilgallon.

ISBN: 979-8215374702

Written by Kathleen Kilgallon.

# Also by Kathleen Kilgallon

**The Tommy and Kindra Series**
Planted


**Standalone**
The Dime Store Joseph

For my sons Joseph and Mason, you inspire me everyday.

Cover Credit~ Designed by Kathleen Kilgallon using Canva.com

Carol cried softly as she looked at the newly acquired Nativity Set, it wasn't much really, just an inexpensive set purchased at the Dime Store. This was the very first Christmas decoration she had purchased since losing every single Christmas item she owned, and she figured the Holy Family was as good a place to start as any.

She moved in closer to get a better look. As was protocol in most Nativity Sets, Mary was as morose as ever, almost as if she could look into the future and foresee the tragic death her son would suffer. Joseph looked perplexed and unsure of what had just happened, and who could blame him, Carol thought. It was, after all, a pretty peculiar thing for your wife to have been impregnated by the Holy Spirit. She peered closely into the Holy Infant's face. He looked chubby-cheeked and healthy with robust pink cheeks and a head full of tousled blond hair. She laughed slightly at the babe having golden hair. She had always assumed he was a dark-haired little fellow given his Middle Eastern heritage, but she supposed anything was possible, even a blond-haired Jesus. As she rubbed the baby's tiny cheek, a tear rolled down her own.

She thought of the Nativity Set that she had so lovingly painted many years ago, each figure carefully coated in bright colors by her own hand. This too was a complete set including the Holy Family, the Wise Men, various farm animals, the mandatory camels, and the barn providing shelter for the weary travelers. She and her ex-husband had worked on assembling the barn together during happier days when her eldest son, who was now twenty-six, was just a boy. She had done the painting, her ex had put on the roof, and together they had built the walls of the barn-like structure. But it was gone now, lost in all the chaos of the last few years. She was not even sure what had become of it; it was just gone. Did somebody else own it? Or did it end up in some landfill somewhere? She had no way of knowing.

It was at that moment that the sense of loss overwhelmed her as she thought about everything she had owned, furniture, appliances, books, and everything else, most of which was lost now, save for a few boxes of pictures. Although, she was grateful for those boxes of pictures, more than anything she dearly wished she had her Christmas tree ornaments, some of which she'd had since she was just a girl. It was the homemade ornaments from her children that pained her the most. Those could never be replaced, they were gone, and the finality of it literally opened up a flood gate of tears inside of Carol. Her shoulders shook from her sobbing, her pain was real, it was palpable and it had taken on a life of it's own.

"Woman, why do ya weep?" a small voice asked her with a slight New York accent.

Carol nearly jumped out of her skin. Her wailing subsided as she looked around the small living room to see where the question had come from. She knew it wasn't her ten-year-old son because he wasn't home, and besides he wouldn't have called her 'woman', at least she hoped not. That would have been almost as odd as the little voice calling out to her in the first place.

She shook her head, shook it again, then again for good measure. One could never shake one's head too many times if one were hearing things, especially things asking her why she was weeping and calling her woman. She knew it was stress, that modern age monster. Yes, it was stress, she wasn't losing her ever-loving mind; she was simply stressed out, and who wasn't? The last few months were finally catching up with her. Suddenly she was hungry, and also glad to have an excuse to leave the living room, she headed out to the kitchen to make herself a sandwich. Just when she thought she was safe, and almost to the kitchen she heard the little voice call out again:

"Woman, whatcha weepin' for? I ain't tryna bother you or nothin', just tryna help ya is all."

Carol turned back toward the living room, squinted her eyes, and there was the little Joseph figure poised at the edge of the Nativity Scene and waiting for an answer. It was then that world went black for Carol-she fainted; she crashed down onto the living room floor and narrowly missed hitting her head on the edge of the coffee table.


Bob


Bob sighed heavily as he made his way out into the chilly morning air, his feet crunching loudly on the dirty snow. To him it was just another day without Marlena, the love of his life for the last five years, who had suddenly decided married life wasn't for her. It was a raw deal for Bob, who did want to be married, and in fact had planned to be married to Marlena until death did they part. But he guessed his feelings didn't matter, at least not to Marlena.

He sighed heavily again, got in his truck and slammed the door. He put the key in the ignition and twisted it, slammed the truck in gear and roared out of the driveway, thinking there would be no Merry Christmas for him this year, just loneliness, loneliness, and just for good measure, another side of loneliness.


Beth


Beth shook her head when she read another text from her mother. Why couldn't she see that she was a good kid? At sixteen she'd never been in any kind of trouble, she didn't drink, she didn't smoke pot, she got good grades, and she had never even been kissed by a boy, never even held hands with one. But her mother only saw what she wanted to see, it had always been that way, and Beth didn't anticipate it changing anytime soon.

The text said, "Come straight home after school, and don't argue about it. I need you to be there when the washing machine repair man comes. You do want clean clothes, don't you?"

Beth's reply was, "Yes, Mom, I'll come straight home." Her mother, satisfied with her response, didn't text back. For the record, Beth never argued with her mother, why would she bother? It was a losing battle. Beth merely suggested things; her latest suggestion had been about getting her driver's license, to which her mother's answer was an emphatic, "No!"

"What do you need a driver's license for?" her mother asked, incensed.

"So I can go places."

"Oh, and where does a sixteen-year-old girl need to go?"

"Well, I could drive myself to school." Beth answered, feeling like that sounded pretty logical.

"Not in my car, you won't."

"I could save up my babysitting money and buy my own car."

Her mother laughed. "You just don't have a clue, do you? Do you realize how much babysitting you'd need to do to buy a car, and then you'd have to insure it too. You don't just buy a car and start driving it," her mother said, rolling her large dark eyes.

Beth felt defeated, it was no use. She wiped the tears from her eyes as she entered the school building, wondering would she ever be free from her mother's grip?

Simon

Simon quickly took off his hat as he got on the school bus, and shoved it in his backpack. He hated wearing that hat, it had a great big pom-pom on it and the kids had taken to calling him Pom-Pom Boy. He had complained to his mother about this, but she seemed unconcerned by it, and insisted there was nothing wrong with the hat, that he in fact looked adorable in it. And besides, she didn't have the money to be buying new hats simply because he didn't like the one he had. When she was a little girl she wore what she was given, and blah, blah, blah. Simon wasn't the least bit impressed by her answer, this was the same woman who was prone to exaggeration. One time she had insisted that she had to walk ten miles to school in the snow. He had questioned her about it; it had seemed a little far-fetched to him, well, actually a lot far-fetched.

"Come on, ten miles? Seriously?"

"Well, maybe it was more like one and a half, but still that's pretty far on a cold, snowy morning when you're only four, don't you think?" his mother asked walking away, which was her way of saying the subject was closed.

Not to him, however, first of all, there was something terribly wrong with a hat that was responsible for the kids calling him Pom-Pom Boy. Second of all, no ten, almost eleven year old wanted to look adorable. Cool, maybe, dope maybe, but adorable, nah, no thank you. You can keep your adorable. Third of all, ever since his mom and dad had gotten divorced, his mother never had any money for anything, not even for a lousy pack of gum. And lastly, he wasn't going to wear that foolish hat, he'd rather get that head cold his mother was always promising him if he didn't keep his head covered. In his young mind he challenged the head cold, getting it would be a symbol of him not bowing to absurd authority, and him finally taking control over his own destiny. It would be worth every sneeze, every sniffle, and every cough.

He came back to reality and looked wearily around the bus. He had no friends on it, the only two kids he could call friends were walkers. He wished he were a walker, then he wouldn't be stuck with all these dopey kids, even if that meant walking through the snow and in the cold. He sighed laboriously and bounced around in his seat on the old rickety school bus.

He thought about his dad and how much he missed him. His parents had been divorced for over a year but it still hadn't gotten any easier, in fact, mostly it seemed harder. The two people he loved most in the world didn't live together anymore, it almost seemed like they hated each other at times and it made his young heart feel sad and confused. He wanted his family again, Christmases together, their vacations on the beach, dinners around the old kitchen table, and to see his dad everyday day, not just be relegated to Saturdays and Sundays. It wasn't normal, at least to Simon, to see someone you were used to seeing every day for only two days a week now.

The only thing he didn't miss though, was the fighting and yelling that went on late into the night, which kept him awake, but still he wished they could have worked it out. He felt they were grown-ups, grown-ups who told him not to fight and yell, and not to call people bad names, but yet, that is just what they did to each other. How was he supposed to follow their advice when they themselves couldn't? It was all too much for his juvenile mind.

A tear crept out of his eye and rolled down his cheek; embarrassed, he quickly wiped it away. He looked around to see if anyone noticed, but he didn't have to look far. In front of him in the next seat sat little Sheila Martin, who was eyeing him curiously, who then stuck out her tongue at him. Simon, never one to miss a beat, returned the favor by promptly sticking out his own tongue, and as an added bonus, he flipped her the bird. Embarrassed by the brazen gesture, she quickly turned back around, and Simon, despite the tears that betrayed him, managed to allow a small smile to escape from his lips.


Carol

Carol came to and cautiously looked around. Everything looked normal. She rubbed the side of her head that had hit the ground. There was a small bump, but nothing major; she supposed it could have been a lot worse. She shook her head confused, what had happened? Then she remembered; the Joseph figure from her Dime Store Nativity Set had asked her why she was weeping. She began to feel woozy all over again at the memory. This time she shook her head vigorously, in an attempt to erase the recollection from her mind, but it was futile, the image of the Joseph figure with his long flowing robe, staff, and full head of dark hair asking her why she was weeping was firmly implanted in her mind. Well, she would tell no one about it, not a soul, and to comfort herself, she chalked it up to stress again. No one could deny that she'd been under extreme stress these past few months. The human mind was a curious thing, and she wouldn't put it past hers to come up with a vision such as what she had just seen. She was all but ready to put the matter behind her, when the small voice asked her the same question, but with a slightly different spin.

"Oy vey," Joseph exclaimed. "Like, I said lady, I ain't tryna bother ya. I just wanna know why ya was weepin is all, and if I can help ya. You modern people are so difficult, got all this modern technology but you can't answer a simple question."

She managed to get herself into a seated position, only to find that Joseph was staring at her with his big dark eyes, waiting for an answer. There would be no answer. Carol, being a fairly intelligent woman and not one inclined to talk to porcelain figures, did the only thing she knew to do; exit the room as fast as humanly possible. With that feat accomplished, Carol lowered herself into one of the kitchen chairs and proceeded to fan herself, wondering if the asylum she was to be placed in would allow Simon generous visiting hours. She could only hope.


Simon

After leaving his dad's, Simon came home feeling every phase of misery; already he missed him. The sadness he felt was more than his years could take, a heart could only hold so much pain. He looked around the small living room he shared with his mother, what a dump, he hated it. His dad lived in a nice clean apartment and had already put up a beautiful Christmas tree, but his mom, just had that dumb Nativity Scene. It looked so cheap, he almost despised it. As he looked more closely, however, he also felt jealousy. The Baby Jesus had both his mother and father with him, for Simon that wasn't an option. He'd always be half a boy, going back and forth between the two houses. He voiced his opinion to the porcelain Jesus, but to his surprise it was Joseph who answered.

"You're so lucky, you know that?" Simon asked pointing at the little Jesus.

"Whatdaya mean? Joseph asked.

Without any thought to the illogicality of it all, Simon answered.

"Well, because he has two parents."

"Last time I checked, so did you," Joseph said shaking his head. Kids these days exhausted him. He felt every last one of them was spoiled.

"Yeah, but mine don't live together."

"So what? What's that got to do with anything? They both love you, right?"

"Yes, but I wish it were like we used to be."

"But kid, be honest with yourself, was it always happy?'

Simon thought carefully about it before before he answered.

"No," he answered truthfully. "But they are grown-ups," he added.

"So?" Joseph asked, wondering where the child was going with all of this.

"So, they should be able to work through all their differences, shouldn't they?"

"Kid, you're livin' in a dream world, I tell ya. Your parents are imperfect people livin' in an imperfect world. Stuff happens..."

Simon, with the realization finally hitting him that he was talking to a porcelain figure, and from the Dime Store no less, decided it was time to wrap up this conversation. Being a practical boy, who didn't waste words, he simply turned around and walked away.

In bed that night as the moonlight crept through his low-cost blinds, he could only think about the whole strange affair, and how his parents were 'imperfect people, in an imperfect world.'


Carol and Simon


Mother and son sat at the dinner table, neither one eating much. Simon pushed his corn around for the tenth time, Carol slowly chewed her chicken. It was rubbery anyway, and she found little enjoyment in it. Both were lost in their own thoughts. Simon was still pretty shaken up from his conversation with the porcelain Joseph figure. He wondered if he had dreamt it, but no, he knew he hadn't. He knew without a doubt that he had had a conversation with that porcelain Joseph with the funny accent. Joseph had certainly given him a lot to think about, but it was little comfort. Why did his parents have to be the ones to get divorced? It was a terrible thought he knew, but he didn't care, why couldn't it be one of his friends whose parents were divorced. They all seemed so happy, so 'in love.' Why did Simon have to be the one with the messed up parents?

Simon pushed his corn over to the other side of his plate, and made a stab at his chicken without putting any in his mouth. His mother, taking a break from her own musing, noticed her son's strange behavior.

"Are you going to play with your food or eat it? I don't think that corn needs to be pushed to the other side of the plate again, do you?" she asked, slightly annoyed.

Simon shook his head no. It was just all so weird, the whole divorce thing and now the Nativity Set Joseph thing. Couldn't he just have an ordinary life?

"Can I be excused?" he asked. "I'm just not hungry."

His mother reached over and felt his forehead. It felt normal.

"Are you okay?" his mother asked, her annoyance turning to concern.

"Yeah, I'm just tired. I think I'm gonna take a little nap."

"All right, sweetie." She watched him turn to leave the kitchen.

She loved that boy more than words could say, and she worried about him constantly. She knew the divorce had been particularly hard on him. It's never what she wanted, nobody got married hoping to divorce, but things happen, and some bridges couldn't be mended once they were broken. But that did little to appease the guilt she felt, guilt a mother feels when she knows her baby is hurting and there's nothing she can do to fix it.

She rubbed her temples, pondering her life, thinking about herself as that naive pregnant eighteen-year-old girl who had such high hopes for the future. When her first son, a sturdy eight-pounder with red hair and big blue eyes, was born, Carol poured herself into motherhood, believing perfection was attainable. They would be the perfect family, Carol would be the perfect mother, and there was nothing her small family couldn't achieve. Then a darkness poked holes in her flawless facade. It reared it's ugly head in moments of anger, in the screaming, in the breaking of household objects, and in the belittling. Carol had chalked it up as normal, but this normal behavior only got worse as the years went on. Finally Carol knew she couldn't do it anymore, the facade had been completely ripped and there was nothing left to hide behind. The perfect family had been exposed as frauds, equal parts shame, equal parts raw vulnerability, and each dealt with the blow in their own way. In the middle of all this was a nine-year-old boy, redheaded like his brother but with deep brown eyes, left to make sense of it all, but without the coping skills of his older family members. A bomb went off in the middle of his family, leaving each one damaged, but none as much as Simon.

Carol sighed, the sigh of one whose dreams had been crushed. She got up; it was time to turn off the memories. They were both painful and happy at the same time, exhausting too. She was already exhausted just from life, no need to make herself more exhausted by digging up memories that were better off left alone.

Also, there was the thing with the porcelain Joseph figure. She was seriously alarmed with the state of her own mental health. When an inanimate object was trying to communicate with you, it was time to be concerned. Maybe she just needed to relax, she was, after all, wound up tighter than a two-dollar watch. Maybe a hot bath? She smiled, when was the last time she had indulged in that luxury? So long ago she couldn't remember. Yes, it certainly couldn't hurt and it just might do her a world of good. But for now she would stay out of the living room, no use inviting trouble. If other inanimate objects started talking to her, then she would know it was time to get help, but for now it appeared as though only PJ (Porcelain Joseph) was trying to communicate with her.

She left everything in the kitchen as it was, too tired to clean it up, and headed into the bathroom to draw her bath. Once the task was completed, she lowered herself into the warm water, and submerged herself. Unable to resist it's alluring pull, Carol was asleep in minutes, only to be awoken by dreams of being chased by PJ demanding to know, "What's wrong with ya, lady?"


Bob


Bob looked around to see if he could find where the leak was coming from. He was in one of his tenant's apartments, who had called him that morning to complain of the leak. She was a new tenant who seemed nice enough and lived there with her boy. They both seemed so sad, the mother and her son. He knew she had recently gotten divorced, and if anyone knew how hard that was, it was him. Thank goodness he and Marlena never had any kids. He couldn't imagine how difficult it would be with children in the picture.

He tried to keep himself busy, really busy. The last place he wanted to be was in that big old house by himself. Everywhere he looked he saw Marlena, in the big leather couch she had picked out, in the floral dishes she had picked out from France, in the high thread-count sheets she had insisted on purchasing (claiming cheaper sheets gave her a rash), in the shower which still contained her Paul Mitchell shampoo and conditioner, and in the basement where her elaborate Christmas decorations were neatly stored. In short he felt like he couldn't escape the woman, it's like these objects were mocking him, teasing him, flaunting at him something he could never have again- the love of his wife. There wasn't even another man involved, the bitter truth was that Marlena simply didn't want him.

He sighed heavily, he had become a big sigher lately. Oh well, there was no use in thinking about all that right now. He could think about it until his brain exploded but it wouldn't change anything, and it certainly was of no benefit to him.

Bob spotted the leak in the corner of the small living room. This was an old house made up of theirs and three other apartments. They lived in a quaint New England mill town, whose heyday was at least a hundred years ago when houses just like this were built to shelter the many French Canadians who crossed the border to work in the mills. Bob was grateful for the houses and the mills because his great-grandfather was one of those French Canadians. He'd come over as a young man of eighteen to find his fortune in the mills, and although he didn't find any fortune, he did find a good wife, which in Bob's opinion was better than any fortune. Grandpa Paquette found his wild Irish rose, Mary Sullivan, a woman with a heart of gold but a temper to match. Bob loved Nana Mary more than words could say, she remained his best friend until she died at the age of 101, still sharp as any tack.

He was grateful for the houses, and owned three of them on the same street. No, they didn't make him rich, quite the opposite. These old homes could be money pits but they kept him busy. In his happier days with Marlena he almost resented them because they took time away from her, but now they were his saving grace.

He did his best with the upkeep, which wasn't easy considering the age of the buildings, but he was a fair and decent human being who believed his tenants deserved to live in safe, sanitary, adequate housing. Many times he toyed with the idea of selling them, but he had formed a personal bond with many of the tenants, some of whom had been with him for over twenty years. He wasn't ready to just hand them over to anyone who wanted to make a fast buck on them. Most landlords these days were all about doing very little for the tenant while trying to charge them a small fortune, but Bob wasn't one of those guys, he wasn't raised that way. He believed in doing his best even if it wasn't reciprocated, not because it was dependent on anyone else, but because he knew in his heart doing the right thing was...well...always the right thing.

His thoughts were everywhere today. He made his way over to the leak relieved to see that it was small, and would be an easy fix. He turned to head out to his truck and get his supplies.

"Pssst," he heard. What the heck, he thought. He was the only one here. His tenant, Carol, had given him permission to be in the apartment when nobody was home. He always asked; he respected his tenants, and went strictly by the book. Deciding he must be hearing things, he set out once again into the cold December air to get the sandpaper, spackle, spatula and small ladder to patch the leak.

Upon returning to the living room he got busy with his work. He nearly fell off the ladder when he heard that "Pssst" again, and this time it was a bit louder. He climbed back down the small stepladder and looked around.

"Hey you, I'm over here," a small voice said.

Someone must be playing tricks on him, he thought. Well, he wasn't amused. He peered around again, still not seeing anything. He decided it must be one of the kid's toys, shrugged it off, and climbed back up the ladder.

"Hey, I'm talkin' to you." The small voice said again.

He looked over to see that the voice was coming from the compact Nativity Set on the shelf. He came back down, again, to get a closer look, and was quite startled to see the Joseph character, animated and looking right at him. He wondered what kind of Nativity Set this was, and thought maybe it was some new interactive kind. He shook his head, he didn't have time for this. He had this leak to repair, a tenant with heating issues, and old Mrs. Beldon with a closet door coming off the hinges. He resumed his work when the porcelain Joseph spoke again.

"Hey, you, I got some things we need to discuss. That all right?"

Bob laughed out loud, what could this porcelain Joseph figure possibly need to discuss with him. Whatever it was, Bob wasn't interested, and quite frankly, no, it wasn't all right. He finished his work and packed up his supplies, intent on ignoring the animated Nativity Set. The little Joseph, however, was making that impossible.

"I know all about ya."

"What?" Bob asked.

This was getting to be a little too much, he thought. When a Nativity Set Joseph claimed he knew all about you, it was probably time to take the batteries out. Well, he was leaving. He would leave Joseph to converse with himself.

"I know your name is Bob." PJ said.

Bob was becoming disturbed, and then he had an idea. Maybe he was on one of those prank shows, if so, his buddies had set this up. He had to admit it was pretty clever. They must have gone to a lot of trouble to set this up, and even got Carol involved. He was a good sport, he'd play along. He looked the little Joseph in the face.

"Well, that was a very good guess, but Bob is a pretty common name." He was curious to see what Joseph would say next.

"That was no guess," he answered, then adding, "Robert Michael Paquette."

Bob laughed at this. So what, he knew his full name. All his buddies knew this. They were going to have to work a little harder if they were going to really prank him. Bob decided to turn the tables on the jokesters, he would ask the little Joseph figure a trick question, one of which none of his buddies would ever know the answer to.

"Who was my very first crush in the first grade?" Bob asked smiling, thinking he had them now.

"Maggie Jean Williams, the little redheaded girl with the big blues who lived next door." PJ answered without missing a beat.

Bob nearly choked on his spit, nobody would know this. Apparently, though, somehow one of his buddies found this out.

"How do you guys ever find this out? I have to admit, I'm impressed."

"Listen buddy, I know all kinds of things. I been around along time, not much I don't know. Every year 'round this time it's the same, she spends all her time with the kid," Joseph said nodding in the direction of Mary and the Baby Jesus.

"I ain't got nothin' else to do. Her and the kid get all of the attention so I fill my time finding out about you goyim. I know you was born on a glorious October morning. October 17, 1970 to be exact, in Worcester, Massachusetts, to Glenda and Robert Paquette Senior. Your mother was in labor for almost twenty hours with ya, and didn't want to have anymore children after that. Eighteen months later your twin sisters Ramona and Roberta were born. Your parents seemed to have a thing for the Robert names." Joseph answered making himself chuckle.

"You got anything to eat?" he asked as an after thought.

"Ahhh, no, I don't," Bob answered a little shell shocked, and suddenly went white, his heart pounding. Nobody would know all this.

"And your mother called you her Li'l Bear until you were ten and finally demanded she stop. That was on a snowy day and you two were the only ones home, and I believe you were drinking hot chocolate at the time."

Robert remembered that day well, he recalled his mother laughing and saying, "Awww, you'll always be my Li'l Bear, but if you'd prefer, I won't call you you that anymore."

The memory made Robert glum, because his mother had passed away two years ago from cancer, and he'd give anything to hear her call him her Li'l Bear again. He missed her terribly, she was always smiling, even on her last day as she lay in that hospital bed riddled with pain, she smiled when Bob came into the room. Bob's eyes filled with tears at the memory.

This whole thing with the Joseph figure was no fun anymore, it was time for him to leave. Bob collected his stuff as quickly as he could, and practically raced for the door.

"Hey buddy, listen to me, will ya? It's not your fault; Marlena's unhappiness has nothing to do with you."

Darn it, Bob thought to himself, he had almost made it to the door, then the porcelain Joseph had to lay this on him. Well, that porcelain figure had another thing coming. Bob was not about to hang around and listen to any more of this. He had had enough, and suddenly he was angry. He stomped over to PJ.

"Okay, don't say another word. I'm leaving."

He ran out the door as fast as he could, there was no way he was giving that Joseph a chance to utter anything else.

In the end it had turned out to be a long torturous day, and when Bob got home he drank more beer than he should have. He didn't care, though. Marlena was gone, and a Nativity Set Joseph had told Bob more about his own life than even he himself knew. He finally passed out on the couch. He awoke the next morning with a hangover and heartache.

He knew the hangover would go away, but he wasn't so sure about the heartache.


Carol


When Carol got home that evening she looked briefly into the living room to make sure the leak was fixed, and it seemed as though all was well in there. Relief flooding through her, she quickly made herself scarce and went into her bedroom to change her clothes.

She still hadn't gone into the living room, and currently, had no plans to. She could happily spend her life avoiding that room. Who wanted to go into a room that made you question your sanity? Not Carol, that was for sure.


Beth


Beth shivered as she walked briskly to her favorite baby-sitting job, fortunately she lived only a few houses down, especially now that she knew how her mother felt about her getting her license.

She used the extra key she'd been given to let herself in. Just as she was taking her jacket off, the bus pulled up. She peeked her head out the door, and smiled at Simon as he got off the bus. Simon returned the smile and waved.

"Hey, kid, how are you?" she asked, ruffling his hair as he walked in the door.

"Okay," he said wearily.

"Long day?" Beth asked sympathetically.

"Boy, was it ever," Simon said, dropping his backpack on the floor and hanging his heavy winter coat on one of the pegs by the door.

"Let's get a snack, then play that new game on your Nintendo Switch."

The snack sounded good but Simon could do without playing the video game. It was in the living room, and like his mother, Simon had been avoiding the living room like a cat avoided water.

"Let me eat my snack first, I'm not sure I feel like playing any video games right now," Simon said, hoping Beth wouldn't push the issue.

"Oh, come on, I've been looking forward to playing this game all day. How about if you bring your snack into the living room, and I play, you can just watch?"

"No, my mother said no more eating in the living room. I guess I make too much of a mess, and she's worried about ants."

This was a surprise to Beth. Carol had never mentioned anything like this to her. Maybe he'd feel like playing after he finished his snack.

"Well, how about a big tall glass of chocolate milk and some peanut butter crackers?"

"Sounds good," Simon said, smiling, relieved that they didn't have to go into the living room. He wasn't about to risk that Dime Store Joseph talking to them. If he was being honest, and pressed to admit it, he had a little crush on Beth. She was so pretty and always so cheerful.

"So, what's new, kid?" she asked, placing his plate crackers in front of him and pouring his milk.

Simon shrugged his shoulders. "Not much," he answered.

"Boy, for a kid who's only a few weeks away from Christmas, you don't seem too excited."

Simon shrugged his shoulders again; he didn't know what to say. He didn't get excited about anything anymore.

"When I was your age, right after Thanksgiving the excitement started. Do you have your tree up?" Beth asked, marching toward the living room.

"Stay out of there." Simon yelled out.

"Why?" she yelled back laughing.

Simon came up behind her and grabbed her arm.

"Because." He said nervously.

"Because, why?" Beth asked turning to face him.

"Because weird things happen in there."

"Like what?" she challenged.

"Trust me, just weird things."

"I'm going in there. I want to see some of these weird things," Beth said. Giggling, she ran in there before before Simon could stop her.

"It looks so peaceful in here, nothing but some furniture, and a sweet little Nativity Set." She picked up the Baby Jesus and cradled him in her hand, then she picked up Mary.

"Look at you Little Mama," she said to the figure, "so proud of your newborn son."

She put them down, and then picked up the Joseph figure.

"Put him down." Simon yelled clearly alarmed.

"Why? What's he gonna do? Bite me with his non-existent teeth?" Beth teased, looking in the little Joseph's face.

"No, he won't bite you, but he can talk!"

"What?" she burst out laughing. "He's just a porcelain figure."

"I know that, but trust me; he talks."

"Oh, yeah, and what exactly does he say?" Beth asked, still amused.

"I don't know, stuff about my parents, stuff like how they're imperfect people in an imperfect world."

This caused Beth to give pause, she was beginning to feel concerned for the boy. Did Simon really believe that the Joseph figure was communicating with him?

"So, the porcelain Joseph counsels you?"

"Kinda." Simon asnswered, embarrassed.

"What else does he say?"

Simon fidgeted around, still embarrassed. "I don't know, he tells me my parents love me. I don't know, stuff like that." He said again, unsure of what else there was to say. He wished he had never said anything to Beth in the first place; now she probably thought he was a nutcase.

Sympathy welled up inside of her for Simon. The divorce must be really tearing him up inside, so much so, that he believed a Nativity Set character was counseling him. Beth knew nothing about divorce, as her own father had taken off when she was just a baby. But she imagined it must be very hard for a kid.

She put the little Joseph back in his spot next to his wife, as Mary continued her vigil looking after her first born son.

"Okay, let's go back into the kitchen." Beth said putting her hand on Simon's shoulder.

"You do believe me that he talks though, right?"

How to answer this? No, she didn't believe him, but she understood how a boy might find comfort in believing that a porcelain Nativity figure was telling him things about his folks, like how they still loved him. She assumed it was something he needed at this moment in his life.

Out of love, Beth said, "Of course, I believe you."

But Simon was too smart. "No, you don't. I can tell by your face."

"Simon I believe you," she said as convincingly as she could. "Now let's go do something else; maybe I can help you with your homework."

Simon wasn't buying any of it. In a moment of bravado he picked up Joseph, and demanded that he speak to them. But Joseph just continued staring at him with that blank look on his face.

"Stop staring at me with that dumb look on your face." Still the little Joseph figure stayed silent. Simon, his frustration building, yelled in PJ's face.

"Talk, you dummy! You know you can, now talk you idiot. Talk, talk, talk, will you?" he screamed and threw Joseph back into the Nativity Set knocking over little Mary in the process. He began crying.

"He talks! I swear he talks." Simon sobbed.

Beth pulled the troubled boy close to her and gently squeezed him in her arms, then led him out to the kitchen and had him sit down.

"Let's just relax and eat our snack, okay? Then maybe we can go for a little walk."

Simon just shook his head, alarmed by his own outburst. They sat there silently for several long moments until Simon asked, "Can we go for our walk now?"

To which Beth replied, "Of course. But we gotta make sure we bundle up good, it's pretty chilly out there."

Beth helped him find his mittens, and when both were sufficiently prepared for the frigid afternoon, they stepped outside and began their silent walk. Simon was exhausted from his meltdown, and Beth was simply at a loss for words.

When Beth lay in bed later that night she couldn't sleep. She was troubled by what she had witnessed that afternoon. Should she tell Simon's mother? Or just let the incident go, and assume he was just a confused child acting out? She decided to let the incident go, and hoped she was making the right decision. If it happened again, she would be obliged to tell his mother.

Simon, for his part, went back to PJ and demanded an explanation. But the porcelain figure offered none. Simon stormed off, angry, confused, and a bit frightened. What if there were something wrong with him? What if he was crazy? But, no, he wasn't crazy, he knew that porcelain Joseph had talked with him. He sank into bed and fell into a dreamless sleep, emotionally and physically spent.


Carol


Carol must have sneezed for the twentieth time that afternoon. She was at home with a miserable cold. She had just gotten off the phone with her older boy, Jack, who lived out near the Boston area now. Jack had seen the best years with her and her ex-husband, but poor Simon had seen the worst.

Simon had been a surprise. Carol and her ex-husband had tried for many years to give Jack a sibling, but their efforts had been in vain. Finally, after many years of crying, praying, begging, Carol gave up. But life was odd at times and unpredictable, just when Carol had made peace with having only one child; she found out she was pregnant. Her sons were fifteen-and-a-half years apart, which led many people to ask if they had the same father.

Jack had promised to come the day after Christmas with his girlfriend for their holiday visit. Carol was glad to hear this, as she missed him terribly.

She got out of bed despite the aching in her bones, and wandered into the kitchen to make some tea in an effort to relieve her congestion. The house was always so quiet when Simon wasn't home. She was glad she had taken the day off from her job as head cashier at the local discount grocery market. It wasn't a prestigious job by any means, but it helped to keep a roof over their heads, and for that she was grateful.

She grabbed the mug that read 'World's best Mom!' Simon had given it to her last Mother's Day. She filled it with water, and placed it in the microwave. Sometimes she felt like the world's worst Mom, but she figured they didn't make a mug saying that. It was just that sometimes she felt like she had failed Simon, he had so many needs and she wondered- was she doing a good filling them? She didn't know, the only thing she did know, was that her head was killing her, and she needed to lie down, like now.

She finished making her tea and pondered the idea of lying down in the living room, which was the only room with cable. It would be nice to watch a movie while she rested. But still, she was hesitant. Would Joseph try to communicate with her again? Should she risk it? No, porcelain figures didn't communicate with people, it just wasn't possible, and to prove that to herself, she would lie on the couch for the first time in two weeks.

She grabbed the clicker from the coffee table, and picked out a movie she'd always wanted to see, but her exhaustion took over and in moments she was asleep.

"Hey, Carol, wake up, will ya?" She stirred slightly, but fell back to sleep.

"Come on, Carol. Sleepy time is all over. I need you to wake up. We got things to discuss." Little PJ yelled out.

When that attempt failed, he yelled at the top off his small lungs, "Carrolll!"

Carol awoke with a start, sitting up, looking around.

"Is that you, Joseph?" she called, her eyes landing on the Nativity Set, finally settling on PJ who was standing near the edge of the shelf now.

He met Carol's gaze. "Yes, it's me. Phew, I didn't think I was ever gonna get you up. You're a heavy sleeper, ya know that? It ain't easy being a little porcelain figure tryna wake up a human."

"What do you want with me?" she asked, more curious than annoyed.

"Every year 'round this time Mary's busy with kid, he gets all her attention. Rather than spend all my time kvetching, I try to do some good."

Carol was confused. What kind of good could a small Nativity Set Joseph do? And what did it have to do with her?

"You look confused," he said. "Listen, it's pretty simple. I spend the holiday season helping people, usually goyim, they seem to need the most help. Mary and the kid don't even miss me, they're too preoccupied with the Wise Men, and besides with all those animals the place stinks anyway. They don't tell you that. You think it's just a cute little scene, but let me tell ya, those animals go to the bathroom everywhere, and it's anything but pleasant."

Carol was even more confused. What was Joseph's point? And how was a porcelain figure able to help her, and what did she even need help with?

"Okay, I get the whole Mary's busy with the kid thing, but Joseph you have to understand it's a little unusual for a Nativity Set figure to start talking to you. And how can you ever help me?"

"Do you know that God can do anything?" he challenged her.

Yes, she supposed she believed that was true, but the events of the last few years had left her faith dried up.

"Remember the excitement you had as child when you believed God could do anything. Remember how you prayed for your dog when he was sick, remember how you prayed for another child, and God answered both of those prayers. Well, thats the kind of confidence you need now, knowing that God loves you and cares about you enough to use any means necessary to help you, even using a clown like me." He chuckled lightly at the last part.

Carol's mind drifted back to the innocence of her childhood when she naively believed everything would turn out just the way she planned. She would be happily married forever, there would never be any divorce, and she would never end up living in a run-down apartment working her tail off at a discount grocery mart. But an ugliness took over in her life, her heart grew cold, and with it many years of drinking and pain. Thankfully, she had kicked the drinking habit, but a lot of the pain still hung on.

"Earth to Carol," Joseph called out to her.

Carol laughed, she had gotten distracted. "So, porcelain Joseph, what do you want with me?"

"To give you shalom."

"Shalom?" Carol asked.

"Yeah, shalom. It means peace.

"How is an inanimate object conversing with someone going to give them peace, quite the opposite I would say."

"Do you know that God can do anything?" he asked again. "Not believe, but know. There's a difference, bubbeleh," he said moving his hands around to emphasize his point

"Well, of course," she stammered. "But you have to admit this whole thing is just a tad bit unorthodox, wouldn't you?"

Joseph shook his tiny head no. "Oy! If you know that; than why couldn't God could use a Nativity Set figure to communicate with you? God spoke to Moses through a burning bush, to Balaam through his donkey, to others through dreams."

"True," Carol said in between sneezes. "But why me?"

"Why not you? You are a mensch, just because some bad things happened to you, doesn't mean you aren't worthy of good things, understand?"

"I guess, I do. But tell me, Joseph, what does 'mensch' mean. I'm afraid I've never heard that term before."

"Don't be afraid; it means someone of noble character. And, that's you, my dear. You don't know how special you are and how much God loves you. Once you realize that, things will change for you. Okay, Carol, I have an unusual request to ask of you." He said putting out his hand.

Carol grew alarmed, as if this whole thing wasn't weird enough, now PJ had an unusual request to ask of her. "What is it?" she asked.

"Come closer," he said, "and take my hand."

"Why?" Carol asked.

"Oy!" Porcelain Joseph said again. These modern people were tiresome.

"Trust me, Carol. Just do it."

Carol nervously approached the little Nativity figure, and took his tiny hand in her own.

"Close your eyes, Carol," he whispered.

She did as she was told, and was immediately transported to another place. She hadn't opened her eyes yet, but she knew she was somewhere else. She could sense it. It was as if every burden had been left behind.

She felt no sadness, only joy. The air even smelled different, sweeter and cleaner, somehow.

"Open your eyes, my dear." Joseph said a little bit louder this time.

Carol opened them slowly, and gasped. Everything was bathed in a golden light, and even the streets were made of gold. There were great big, glorious mansions ornately decorated, surrounded by blue fountains, and fields of wildflowers growing in every shade of the rainbow. The people walking along the golden streets looked as stunning as she imagined angels would. The beautiful figures didn't seem to notice Carol or Joseph.

"Is this heaven?" Carol asked, breathlessly turning to face Joseph. But this wasn't the little porcelain Joseph figure anymore, but rather a full-size man. He looked just like the figure, only a lot larger, and a lot older. Carol figured he must have been doing this Nativity gig for awhile now, as he looked to be quite elderly.

"Yes, it is. I get up here a few times a year, usually around the holidays. I always enjoy it, sometimes I even run into, well you know who."

"You mean God?"

"Yep, the one and only. We schmooze for a bit, he gives me my assignment for the next year, ya know stuff like that. Anyway, I didn't bring you up hear to talk about me. Take my hand."

She took it and they walked through the streets of heaven hand in hand. Carol smiled at people as they walked past, but nobody seemed to notice the pair.

"They can't see us?" she asked.

"No," he answered. "This is just for you."

They passed a woman who looked like her grandmother, Carol turned around and the woman turned until they were both looking at each other. Carol drew in her breath sharply, it was her grandmother. She looked so young and lovely with her auburn hair cascading down her shoulders. Carol had only seen her white hair, but she recalled many times her grandmother had said, "Why, when I was young, I had the most beautiful red hair." Well, she hadn't been lying; her hair was indeed beautiful.

"Nana, it's me, Carol," she yelled out. Joseph held her back as she got ready to run over and hug her.

"Remember, she can't see you."

"She's looking right at me," Carol said, but even as she spoke the words, Nana turned around and walked away.

"Don't worry, someday she will see you, and you'll never be separated again. But right now, this is what I want you to see," Joseph said as he led her to a spectacular little castle. Then he covered her eyes with his hands and continued to guide her.

"Where are we going?" she asked excitedly.

"You'll see." He promised.

When they arrived at their destination, he removed his hand. Carol gasped, she was inside the miniature castle. It was lavishly decorated in cream and gold colors with splashes of pink here and there. Pink was her favorite color and the wee mansion looked as if it was decorated just for her, but what really caught her eye was the breathtaking Christmas tree that was in front of her. It was the most glorious, magnificent thing she had ever laid eyes on. It went from floor to ceiling, adorned with diamonds, rubies, sapphires, emeralds, and great big, golden bulbs that hung from each branch. The gems dazzled her eyes as they sparkled and shimmered in the white lights that lit up the tree.

"Take a closer look," Joseph whispered in her ear. "I know how some of you goyim love your Christmas trees."

She moved in closer, unsure of what goyim meant, but was quickly distracted when she saw all her precious ornaments she had collected over the years hung on the tree as well. The porcelain angels, birds, snowmen that she had purchased as a little girl from the Christmas Ornament Club she had belonged to, paying for them with her own babysitting money in anticipation of when she would someday have a Christmas tree of her very own. Then she spied the beautiful Candy

Cane Fairy, the very favorite of all her childhood ornaments. She touched the fairy's soft brown hair, and looked into her blue eyes, just like she had as a twelve-year-old girl. She rubbed her satiny, candy cane striped dress and touched her flimsy wings, and a tear rolled down her cheek. The Candy Cane Fairy had graced Carol's Christmas tree for over thirty years; Carol had assumed she was gone forever, and here she was on Carol's forever Christmas tree in heaven.

But as wonderful as the Candy Cane Fairy was, she nothing compared to what Carol saw next: all of the precious homemade ornaments made by her children over the years. There was the paper bell, colored green by her son Jack's own hand, with his smiling preschool picture in the center. She turned it over and saw that he had proudly signed it Jack-Jack, his boyhood nickname. There was Simon's handprint from kindergarten, there were a plethora of Santa's made by the boys over the years with the mandatory cotton ball beards, ornaments made of clay, Nativity ornaments made in Sunday School, Jack's 'Baby's First Christmas' ornament dated 1995, and Simon's dated 2011. Every single ornament made by her sons were hanging from this dazzling tree.

"Oh, Joseph," she said softly, covering her mouth. She turned to look at him, he smiled at her.

"I thought these were gone forever," Carol said pointing at the ornaments. "My husband... things got bad... I had to leave my old house, I put all my stuff in storage... and I couldn't pay my storage fee," she said between sobs. "So all my stuff was sold... I thought I would never see my beloved Christmas ornaments again... especially the ones made by my children. It broke my heart to realize that my cherished, personal Christmas decorations were sold to a stranger who could not care less about how much these meant to me. I felt so violated and powerless knowing there was nothing I could do about it." She began to cry harder.

Joseph held her until the torrent subsided, then wiped her tears with his robe. When she finally calmed down, she looked around.

"So, this is really where I'm going to live when I go to heaven?" Carol asked smiling.

Joseph nodded his head yes, but then turned her face toward his. "But alls I wanted you to see for now was the Christmas tree, the rest is a surprise for you, for later, when heaven becomes your permanent home."

Carol started weeping once more and said, "Thank you, Joseph, thank you," over and over again, and kissed his cheek repeatedly.

Joseph blushed embarrassed by all the attention being showered on him. "Okay, Okay," he said. "You know I'm a married man, right? What would Mary say? She's a good woman, and one heck of a mother, but she has a little bit of a temper too at times. She'd wonder who is this goy with the chutzpah to be kissing on my husband like this."

Carol laughed through her tears. "Can you please tell me what goy means, Joseph?"

"Goy is a non-Jew, two or more non-Jews is goyim. Capeesh?" he asked. "See, I know Italian too, and you're learning Yiddish!"

"Capeesh," she answered laughing again.

"All right, Carol, now do you know that God can do anything?" he asked her.

"Yes, Joseph, I do."

"Okay, then I think we're done here. Ready?" he asked putting out his hand.

"I'm ready," Carol said grabbing his hand.

Joseph led her out again, covering her eyes, and in a few seconds he said, "Carol open your eyes."

She opened her eyes and saw that she was in her living room once more. Joseph winked at her and said, "Okay, kiddo, that was fun. Time for me to get back to the Manager. I gotta make sure them Wise Men ain't gettin' to friendly with Mary, they have a tendency to do that at times, gotta show 'em who's boss," he said cracking his knuckles. And, before Carol could say anything, Joseph was back to being a porcelain figure standing beside his wife at the Nativity Scene.

Carol sighed, but not the sigh of an unhappy person, but the sigh of someone who had just had the experience of a lifetime. Carol's sadness had disappeared, and for the first time, in a very long time, Carol felt peace flood through her and course through her veins. It was surely the best feeling ever.


Bob


Bob was feeling restless. He couldn't keep his mind on his work, which was very unusual for him, more often than not, work was his place of escape. But as he went from one tenant request to the next, he found he kept messing up.

At the Rodriguez apartment he brought in the wrong supplies, instead of paint he carried in tools to fix the plumbing. The plumbing issue was at Mrs. O'Coin's.

"Come on, old man, get yourself together," he chided himself.

Things only got worse at Mrs. O'Coin's, rather than fix the clog in the drain, he ended up flooding the kitchen.

"Lord in heaven," the old lady said as she saw the mess he made.

"Don't worry, Mrs. O'Coin, I'll have this place cleaned up in jiffy." His jiffy turned out to be much longer; over an hour later he still hadn't fixed the problem.

"You sure you know what you're doing?" she asked wide-eyed and alarmed.

"Well, of course, I do," he said trying to make light of it. "I was born knowing how to plumb." The elderly woman eyed him suspiciously, maybe he was on drugs. It seemed like all the kids were nowadays.

At that moment, the professional plumber he had hired knocked at the door. Bob rushed to let him in.

"Okay, this is Stan. He's going to take over from here. Don't you worry, Mrs. O'Coin, you're in good, capable hands. Isn't that right, Stan?" Bob asked smiling.

Stan shook his head. Mrs. O'Coin shook hers too, definitely drugs she thought.

"I'll square up with you later." Bob whispered to Stan, and raced out the door.

"What is wrong with you, old man?" he asked himself aloud as he started his truck.

He knew what it was; he needed to see that cheaply made Joseph figure from the Dime Store Nativity Set. The words of the porcelain figure went round and round in his mind. He remembered distinctly the little voice telling him about his first crush, how his mother called him her L'il Bear, his twin sisters, but what Bob was most interested in was what he had to say about Marlena.

He guessed deep inside of himself, he always knew Marlena was unhappy, and try as he might, he could never make her happy. But maybe the porcelain Joseph could help him; he wanted to pick his brain for awhile. Maybe he knew the secret to making Marlena happy. All at once, he was desperate to see the Joseph figure. He knew he must see him as soon as possible. Maybe, just maybe, he could win her heart by Christmas, and it would be a merry one after all.

His mind raced with possible scenarios, he could call Carol and tell her he needed to do an inspection, or possibly that he needed to check the leak and make sure it was holding up well. Or, maybe say that the other tenants were complaining about an ant problem and he wanted to make sure it wasn't spreading to her place. Nah, ant problems were usually a warm weather issue, and the weather was anything but warm lately.

He knew all this was crazy, really crazy; a fifty-one-year-old man trying to think of any excuse to talk to a porcelain figure. But Bob didn't care, he just had to talk to Joseph.

Beth

Beth walked to the stores downtown to do a little Christmas shopping. She only had two people to buy for, Simon and her mother. Simon, being a huge Patriots fan, would be easy to buy for. She already knew what she was getting him - a new winter hat with a beautiful Patriots logo. She knew how much he hated that other hat he wore. Beth could sympathize, her mother had always made her wear the most hideous clothes, and there was nothing she could do about it. "You don't appreciate anything, do you?" her mother would say. Yes, she appreciated a lot of things, but being picked on by the mean kids at school just wasn't one of them.

Her mother, well, she was another story. Every year it was the same thing, her mother disliked her Christmas gift, and she didn't bother to hide it. Beth sadly recalled last year; she had put a lot of thought into her mother's gift, a lovely silver bracelet with a shell motif. Her mother adored the ocean, so one would surmise a shell bracelet would be appreciated. It had cost her sixty dollars, which to Beth was a good chunk of change. She remembered the look on her mother's face when she pulled the delicate bracelet out of it's festive packaging. Scrunching up her face, she said, "Silver? You know I never wear silver." Then she put it back in it's box, and tossed it under the Christmas tree, where it stayed until Beth grabbed it and stuck it in one of her own drawers.

She wiped away a tear as she entered Maggie's Odds and Ends, a cool little store filled with rare finds. Maggie herself was from Ireland and was as interesting as her finds.

"Whatcha lookin' fer, dear? Anythin' special?"

Beth looked around as she answered, "Something for my mother." Nothing, however, caught her eye.

"Fer yer Ma, is it?" Maggie asked, sensing that the poor girl was confused. "They sure can be difficult, can't they? I have one of me own back in the old country, and I think she's liked mebbe one out of the hundreds of gifts I've given her over tha years. Wish I had me money back that I've spent, Mary and Joseph, I could buy meself a small castle with it, I could." Beth smiled, Maggie had a natural way of making people feel understood.

They stood quiet for a moment before Maggie asked, "Well, is she religious at all? All me religious merchandise is over here," she said pointing to a corner. She then picked up a Joseph statue. "What about a Joseph figure, tis hard to find fault with that."

Beth had to admit it was pretty cool looking, but she knew her mother would have no part of it. She shook her head no.

Maggie laughed. "Ya might wanna try it. I swear tha only gift me Ma did like was the Joseph figure I gave her a few years ago. I believe, I do, that she had a crush on the old boy, and who wouldn't? He was always so noble leading his pregnant wife around, and the babe wasn't even his, ahhhh, an ancient love story with a modern twist, Right?"

Maggie continued, "Me Ma was pregnant with me by some clown but tha man who raised me wasn't me Da."

Beth couldn't relate to any of this, but Maggie was just so entertaining and endearing, that it didn't matter. Beth finally spoke again. "No, my mother isn't religious at all."

"Okay, me love, how about one of these lovely hat and scarf sets knitted in Ireland by hand. Everyone likes to be warm, right? They're so lovely even a Ma would love 'em."

Without saying anything Beth went over and checked out the hat and scarves, she rubbed the soft material between her fingers. She had to admit they were pretty nice. The emerald green set caught her eye the most; she could picture her mother's beautiful face cradled between the hat and scarf.

It was only $28 which Beth didn't think was bad at all considering the quality. She knew it was the perfect gift, and if her mother didn't like it, she could live with it because she knew she had done her best.

"I'll take this." Beth said holding up the hat and scarf set.

"Tis lovely, a lovely choice fer sure. If yer Ma doesn't like it, well, she must be blind." Maggie said, laughing. "But ya know what? I think she's gonna love it."

Beth handed her three tens and happily told her to keep the change. She walked out of there feeling like she had just hung the moon.

But when Beth got home later that day, all her mother did was belittle her.

"You burned the chicken."

Make your own damn chicken.

"Did you even brush your hair today? It looks like some kind of rat's nest."

Of course I did; sorry I'm not as perfect as you.

"Beth, Beth, Beth, you don't have a clue, do you? When you grow up and leave here, you're going to get swallowed up because you have no grasp on reality."

I'm trying, but you erode every little bit of confidence I do have. At that point Beth just wanted to throw the lovely hat set right into the garbage, but instead she went up to her room to escape.


Bob


As luck would have it, Bob didn't need an excuse to enter Carol's apartment. Carol called him that evening and asked if tomorrow he could come by and check the stove, for the oven didn't seem to be reaching temperature properly.

He smiled into the phone and said, "I'll be there first thing in the morning."

Simon

Simon had been home for almost an hour now, and still he didn't feel any better. His mother was napping, and he was just wandering around the living room feeling sorry for himself. He had had a great weekend with his dad, they went to the movies, his dad bought him a new video game, and took him for ice cream. But now he was back in this dumpy place, which definitely wasn't as big and as nice as his dad's. It was small and dark, and the little bit of furniture they did have was mostly second hand. Plus, his mother never took him any place; he'd ask, but the answer was always the same, "I'm sorry, Simon, I just don't have the money for that." Well, his dad did, so why didn't she?

He sat on the couch and began to cry. He hated his life. He picked up the clicker from the coffee table and threw it across the room. It hit the Dime Store Joseph squarely in the head, and he went crashing to the floor. Simon raced over to see if the Joseph was okay. He picked him up and miraculously the Joseph figure remained unscathed. Relieved, Simon exhaled loudly.

"Yeah, I'm fine, kid, but next time ya might wanna try punchin' a pillow or somethin'. You could've taken my head off." PJ said angrily.

At this point Simon wasn't all that fazed by the verbal figure, in fact he had a question for him. "How come you didn't talk that day when Beth was here? She probably thinks I'm crazy."

"Because I didn't need to. I'm not some side show freak here for your amusement. I only talk when necessary."

"So it wasn't necessary to keep someone from thinking I'm nuts?"

"No, it wasn't, and besides, she doesn't think you're nuts. Anyway, listen, kid, we got more important things to discuss."

"Like what?" Simon asked, annoyed.

"Like you."

"What about me?" Simon asked, still holding Joseph in his hand.

"Kid, you got all kinds of issues from your folks divorce. Divorce is never easy for anyone, especially for someone your age, but I can help you, if you give me the chance."

"I don't wanna work on anything. I wanna be left alone. My parents should work on things, not me. I'm just a kid."

"True enough, but they're old, and not gonna change. You're young, and if we don't fix you now, you're gonna end up with all kinds of hang ups, and be just as miserable as you are now for the rest of your life. I don't think you want that, do you?"

Simon didn't know what to say, but he knew he didn't want to be miserble for the rest of his life. So he asked the Dime Store Joseph what he needed to do.

"Okay, kid, give me your hand."

"Why?" Simon asked, confused.

"You wanna be miserable or not, that's the real question. If you don't; take my hand and don't ask anymore questions. Capeesh?"

Simon clutched the tiny porcelain hand in his own, and in an instant he was in his old kitchen. His mother and father were there and they were fighting.

"Carol, I can't deal with your- blankety, blankety, blankety, blank- anymore." it was all obscenities as his father screamed at his mother.

"Well, maybe things would be different if you hadn't gotten yourself that whore," she screamed back. His father headed for the door, but his mother could never shut up, she could never leave things alone. She always had to follow him. Many times Simon wanted to yell at her, "Can't you ever just shut up? Why do you always make things worse with your mouth?" But he already knew the answer to that, It was the bottle, which made her combative. He dreaded the days when she drank because it usually lead to a confrontation between his parents, and many times those confrontations got violent. As his father stepped outside his mother yelled a bunch of expletives at him, until finally he charged back into the house and grabbed her by the arm. He pulled her inside, then pushed her down, and then grabbed her by the shoulders and shook her. Still she continued to taunt him, "Oh, you're such a man, pushing a woman down."

Simon started crying. "Just stop it you two, just stop it," he said through tears, but it was as if they didn't even hear him. His father kept squeezing his mother's shoulders and shaking her, her head hitting the floor.

"Dad, please," Simon yelled, but the troubling scene continued. "It's me, Simon, your son. I'm here, please stop this you two, please just stop it," he cried.

Finally, Joseph, now a full-sized man, grabbed Simon's hand and led him away from the horrible scene. He pulled him in for a hug, and simply let the child cry. Simon cried until his tears were spent, and in between sobs he yelled, "Why? Why?"

Before he knew it, he was back on his beat up old couch wiping his tears away. The tiny Joseph figure was seated beside him now.

"What was all that about?" Simon asked.

"Listen, kid, you needed to see that, as painful as it was. You need to stop romanticizing the past."

Simon looked him. "Huh?" he asked.

"You know, making it seem better than it was." Joseph explained, figuring the kid probably didn't know what "romanticize" meant.

"You cry for the good ol' days, but them good ol' days wasn't always so good. Your parents went down a road that few people can ever come back from. They created gulf between themselves that neither could cross. I'm afraid if they stayed together, the ending would have been worse than divorce." Simon's eyes got wide at that and he became afraid.

"Don't be afraid, kid. Everything's gonna be okay now. God can use all these broken pieces in our lives to make something beautiful out of it. And, neither of your parents are bad people, but what they created was something so toxic it had to come to a close. "

"But, why did it have to be my parents?" Simon still wondered.

"Who knows, only God does. But the point is Simon, you're gonna be all right. You're gonna go on to lead a happy life, not a perfect one, nobody has that, but a good one. Now, let me see a smile on that adorable little punim."

Simon smiled in spite of himself, and in spite of not knowing what "punim" meant. Joseph certainly used some strange words.

Joseph laughed, "Your face, punim is your face."

The whole experience was exhausting for Simon, but it had liberated him as well. He no longer carried the burden of wondering, wondering if somehow his parents could have made it work. He knew now they couldn't, and it was time for him to accept it, and with acceptance came peace.

They heard his mother in the bathroom. "Okay, Simon, put me back at the Manger Scene." Simon quickly did as he was asked before his mother came into the living room.

"Whatcha doing, kiddo?" she asked smiling.

"Nothing, just getting ready to watch some TV."

"Let's go get a pizza, then go get our tree."

"Really?" Simon asked surprised, his mother hardly ever offered to get a pizza.

"Yeah, now get your shoes," she said laughing, "before I change my mind."

Simon smiled and grabbed his shoes, while his mother put on her coat. He looked over at PJ, and the little porcelain figure winked at him. Simon no longer hated his life.


Bob


Bob could hardly contain his excitement as he drove to Carol's apartment. He realized that this was possibly the strangest thing he had ever done, but he didn't care. He needed to talk to that Dime Store Joseph.

He arrived at Carol's full of questions for PJ. Maybe after their time apart, Marlena would be ready to reconcile. She'd see, he was sure, that he was man for her, that nobody could love her like he could. He wanted to ask Joseph when all this would happen. He figured that's why Joseph had reached out to him in the first place, to tell him, that although Marlena was confused, she'd come around, ready to resume their life together.

He raced over to the Nativity Set only to find that the Dime Store Joseph was nowhere to be found, where would he go? Did the Joseph figure walk, too? He looked on the floor, on the shelves, he looked at Mary and the Babe as if they could tell him, but they remained as silent and as still as ever. He looked under the couch, under the tree, he looked everywhere, until he was frantic. He ran around the house calling out, "Joseph, oh, Joseph, where are you?" But the little Joseph remained missing in action. He gave it one more shot, yelling out, "Joseph" as loud as he could. But there was no answer.

Bob was crestfallen. What had happened to Joseph? He sat on the couch to get his thoughts together, realizing that he still had that stove to fix. He figured it was his own foolish fault, was he really expecting a porcelain Joseph figure to tell him that Marlena was going to come running back to him, declaring her undying love? What a moron he was. He supposed it was for the best that he hadn't seen porcelain Joseph. Joseph would probably tell him what a clod he was, and he'd be forced to agree.

He got to work on the stove, shaking his head. "Really, Bob" he said aloud to himself, "Talking to a Joseph figure from a Nativity Set?" He needed his head examined, that's what he needed.

He spent the rest of the day nervous and agitated about himself, about Marlena, about life. "Dammit, Bob, get yourself together," he chided himself in bed that night.

Beth

Beth arrived early to babysit Simon with her head all a mess. She was feeling so enraged at her mother, she literally wanted to smack her right in her smug face. Feeling this way was a rarity for Beth, she usually took her mother's belittling all in stride, but not this time. Now, she felt as if she just couldn't take it anymore.

She read again the text her mother had sent to her on the way home from school:

"I'm so sick of your laziness, not to mention selfishness. The only thing I asked you to do this morning was clean the bathroom before you left for school and guess what??? I came home on my lunch break to find you haven't lifted a finger!!! Not one!!! It's just as dirty as when I left this morning. Did you think I wouldn't notice??? You're a very ungrateful young lady. You'd better get it done TONIGHT unless you want to be grounded for a week!!!"

The anger was boiling over inside of Beth, and she called her mother every rotten name she could think of.

"And for your information, mother, I didn't have time to clean that stupid bathroom this morning. I've been up since four o'clock studying for my calculus exam and finishing my biology report, because if I get a bad grade, you'll say I'm dumb and don't try hard enough. All I do is try hard, hard to please you and it's never enough. I'll never be good enough to live up to your impossible standards, you can't even live up to your own standards, nobody can. And if you're so worried about it, why don't you get off your own lazy butt and clean the bathroom yourself!" Beth ranted loudly.

Beth surprised herself with the intensity of her own emotions, but for once in her life she didn't care. She hoped her mother heard her, she hoped the whole world heard her. She had bottled up her emotions for far too long.

"I can't stand you, I can't stand you, I can't friggin stand you, and I never want to see your miserable face, not ever again." She screamed into the silent living room. She got up and kicked the couch. "I was going to clean that dumb bathroom tonight, you know?"

In the middle of her rage she heard a little voice call out, "Beth." She hoped it wasn't Simon, she had probably scared the daylights out of him. He was the one person she didnt want to see her like this. Suddenly, her rage was gone, and she felt only shame.

"Simon, it's okay. I was just mad at my mother. I'm not mad at you, and I'm fine now." She called out, but there was no answer. She ran around the apartment in search of him but he was nowhere to be found. She looked outside, but still no Simon. She went back inside and realized it was only 2:30, Simon wasn't due home until at least 3:00. She shook her head, she must have imagined it then.

She sat on the couch and took a deep breath, then grabbed the book she was reading for her English Literature class out of her backpack. No use thinking about her mother anymore; it wouldn't change anything.

"Beth," she heard again, but this time it sounded like a man's voice, one that was very faraway. "Over here," it called out.

If Beth wasn't mistaken, it sounded like it was coming from the little Nativity Set. Was someone playing games with her? She got up and walked towards it, and to her amazement it was the Joseph figure. He was standing on the edge of the shelf looking at her expectantly.

"So, you do talk?" she asked almost annoyed.

"Yeah, listen, I do. The kid wasn't goin' crazy or nuthin'. I only talk when necessary though and never on command. I ain't someone's show pony, I got important work to do."

"Like what?" she asked, this time she was amused.

"Like help you, princess. You got issues, although, I will say you deal with them very well. I'm impressed with the way you handle your mother. Most kids would have rebelled, ran away, got drunk, slept with Frankie down the street, or flipped their mother off at the very least, but not you kid. You're a class act all the way."

Beth was left speechless, nobody had ever said anything this kind to her. She was almost a little alarmed, maybe the stress of living with her mother was taking it's toll, and she was imagining things.

"Okay, can ya do me a favor and get me off this shelf? Mary's starting to stare, she gets weird sometimes."

Beth picked him up gently. "Okay, princess, I have another favor to ask of you; take my hand, and for the love of all that's holy, don't ask why, just do it. Capeesh?"

Beth grabbed his hand not knowing what to expect. "Close your eyes," the litte Joseph whispered. Beth closed her eyes hoping she wasn't about to wake up in a mental hospital.

"Can I open them?" she asked, her voice small.

"Go for it, princess, and don't be afraid; this is all for your benefit."

When Beth opened her eyes, she was in her grandmother's kitchen back in Southie, in the old Irish neighborhood of South Boston. She saw her mother as young girl of maybe eight, and her grandmother sitting at the table. It was a strange scene, though. Her mother had a great big pile of potatoes in front of her which she appeared to be peeling, while her grandmother was talking and laughing into the phone. Her mother looked unhappy as she continued her chore. When Grandmother Donovan finished her conversation, her demeanor suddenly changed.

"You're not done yet?" her grandmother demanded angrily of her young daughter. The child just shook her head no.

Wondering what was going on, Beth looked over at the full-size Joseph. Surprised to see him standing next to her as a full-grown man complete with a beard, and wrinkles around his eyes on his weather-worn skin.

Her surprise wasn't lost on Joseph. "Yeah, kid, I'm old. I been doing this whole Mary and the Baby Jesus gig for a long time." He said stressing the word 'long.'

Beth didn't say anything as her attention was quickly drawn back to the episode in the kitchen.

"Don't you shake your head at me, young lady. I don't understand why this is taking you so long. You've been at it nearly thirty minutes and you have three peeled, THREE! You are an incredibly lazy girl, not to mention selfish. Don't you understand we are having company tonight and I NEED these potatoes peeled, and then you are to mop the kitchen floor, and then vacuum and dust the living room. Are you getting this? Is anything getting through your impossibly thick skull?" Grandmother asked, knocking on her daughter's head.

Beth shook her in disbelief; it seemed like an awfully tall order to ask of one so young. When the girl didn't answer, Grandmother Donovan got even more aggressive, pulling Beth's mother's face toward her own.

"You answer me right now, young lady, before I smack the stupidity right off your homely little face.

"Answer her," Beth yelled out, but they were invisible to the mother and daughter. "Do something, Joseph." She demanded of him, but Joseph just shook his head no, and put his finger to his lips to silence her.

"Keep watching," he whispered.

"Yes, mother, I'm sorry. I'll go faster, I promise." The child said, finally speaking, clearly afraid.

"You'd better, or trust me, young lady; you'll be sorry." Grandmother Donovan called, heading toward the bathroom. "I'm going to take a much needed bath after all your nonsense, and when I step out of the bathroom, every single potato better be peeled, and your little behind better be mopping that kitchen floor, got it?"

Her mother shook her head. "Don't shake your head, I asked you a question. Either you got it or you don't."

"Yes, mother, I got it." Her mother answered, crestfallen and defeated. Beth wanted to hug her mother but Joseph held her back.

It's time to go," he said gently.

"But, but, my mother needs me." Beth cried.

"Listen, bubbeleh, as hard as that was to watch, there's nothing you can do about it. Now take my hand," he said gently. She did, and in an instant they were transported back to Simon and Carol's living room. Beth sighed heavily as she replayed the scene in her mind. Her emotions went from sorrow, to anger, to shock. To see a young child treated so horribly by someone who was supposed to love them left a bad taste in her mouth.

She looked for Joseph, he was seated on the couch back to being a porcelain figure again. Quiet sobs escaped from Beth, she felt so sorry for the young girl in the scene. Nobody deserved to be treated like that, especially a child. The sobs grew louder as she thought about the way her mother treated her. She and her mother shared that pain, being treated so severely by the one you loved most, and who was supposed to love you and protect your heart from cruelty, but yet, was the one who was the perpetrator, the one who hurt you the most.

PJ finally spoke. "You saw something important today, you saw your mother vulnerable. You've only seen her as the big bad wolf, but she was once just a young girl just like you, looking for love, looking for approval; she never got any. So, I'm afraid, that's the only way she knows how to love. But, listen, bubbeleh, you're different, you're special. Take that pain and use it for good, your heart is still kind. I need you to spread love in this world, especially to your mom, she needs it the most. In her heart she's still that little girl, and in her pain, she takes it out on the one she loves most- you. One day, you'll see her vulnerable again, I promise, and she'll apologize in her own way. Now put me back by the Nativity Set, I can see the kid is crying, Mary's frustrated and looking for me. I can usually soothe the kid singing from the Psalms, although my voice sucks, but the kid seems to like it."

Beth picked up the little figure and placed him by Jesus. Joseph winked at her, ready to again be part of his little family. Beth looked around, dazed and confused. She started to cry; it was a release more than anything. She saw things that made her so sad, but she also had

Joseph's words of encouragement too. She did what she always did, she drew upon that strength that lived within her, she was never down for long, and she wouldn't be now. She got ready, soon Simon would be home. She'd be that perky cheerleader babysitter he needed.

"Hey, Kid want a snack?" she asked smiling. he shook his yes, it was at this moment Beth knew everything would be all right.

Bob

It was two days before Christmas and Bob was feeling even more depressed than usual. He had never experienced loneliness like he had in these past few weeks. His sister, who lived in New Hampshire, had invited him to spend the holiday with her family, but he just didn't think he could do it. Seeing a happy family would only remind him of what he didn't have. At home he could wallow in his misery, drink too much, and pass out. It was just too much effort to put on a happy face and act festive, plus she had young children and he was afraid his bad attitude would frighten them, and they might end up calling him Uncle Scrooge.

Just then his cellphone rang, it was Carol. She hated to bother him, but could he please stop by and check the stove once more. It appeared the old stove was failing to reach the correct temperature again. Bob agreed and told her he'd come over right now since today was a slow day, and he'd fix it right this time or spend the whole day trying. Bob was a perfectionist who got easily upset with himself when he failed to fix something the first time.

The apartment was quiet, and Bob quickly got to work on the troublesome stove. He turned it on, setting it to 350, and while he waited, he checked his phone, but had no messages.

"Hey, Bob, I need to talk to ya, ya got a minute?" a little voice called out.

"Oh, no, not this again." Bob said out loud. Well, he had news for that little Joseph, he wasn't about to go anywhere near that Nativity Set. He could call out all he wanted but Bob would remain adamant.

"Oh, come on, Bob; be mature about this. No time to be a child anymore. I got stuff to tell ya. Come on, ya know wanna hear it."

Bob feeling every bit like a defiant child, yelled out, "No!"

"Bob, come on now, don't be a eyngeshparter."

"A what?" Bob yelled out. As if this wasn't already weird enough, couldn't the Joseph figure at least use words Bob understood.

"A stubborn person, now get your tuchus over here, Bob. We got work to do."

Okay, fine, he wouldn't be whatever that word was. He marched over to the Joseph ready to listen to him, or maybe fight him. It could go either way.

"I was here, where were you last time? I called for you, no response, dude. I'm not down for games. I'm too old."

"Precisely my point, now, no disrespect, but shut up and take my hand. And, FYI I was around, but listen, I got my own schedule, I can't always work around you goyim. Either you wanna find out about Marlena or you don't. Brother, it's that simple. Take my hand," Joseph said offering his hand.

Against everything in him, he did just that; he took Joseph's hand. But he was angry, angry at, well, everything, especially himself. He was a gullible fool. What grown man took a porcelain figure's hand? Him, he was that gullible fool.

In a moment Bob could tell they were someplace different. He didn't know how or why he knew, but he knew.

"Open your eyes, Bob," PJ said.

Bob did as he was told, immediately wishing he hadn't. He opened them to see Marlena and a good-looking young man seated at the table of a fancy restaurant.

"What's this all about?" he asked a full-size Joseph.

"You'll see, just keep watching." Joseph answered calmly.

Bob swallowed hard and watched Marlena smile at the man, this was proving almost impossible to watch. Bob could only surmise that Joseph was trying to torture him, especially as the man grabbed her hand and brought it to his lips, and placed a gentle kiss on it. He then proceeded to lead her to the elegant dance floor, where he held her close and kissed her again, this time on the cheek. Bob had seen enough; he wasn't going to hang around and wait and see if the guy was about to plant one on her lips.

"I'm ready to go." He said grabbing Joseph's hand. "Get me out of here."

"Not so fast. We're not done here yet."

"Well, I got news for you, buddy; I am!"

"Bob, Bob..." Joseph started to say.

But Bob didn't let him finish, in a rush of passion and anger he raced over to the couple yelling, "Marlena what's he got that I don't have? I didn't know you wanted to go dancing, I would have taken you dancing. I would have done anything for you, anything," he screamed.

Joseph grabbed him and pulled him back. "They can't see or hear you."

"So, this is what you wanted me to see so bad? My wife, yes, she's still MY wife," he said angrily, "being wined and dined by some clown, and he has the nerve to kiss her. She told me she need this time to herself, doesn't look like it to me.

"She does, Bob. But women are curious creatures, particularly this one. And I thought Mary had her oddities; one minute Mary says she tired of those Wise Men always hanging around every year, next thing I know, she's laughing and flirting with them. But I can say, I ain't never seen her dancing with any of them, so I think Marlena's got her beat."

This did little to comfort Bob. He shook his head and hoped the misery would be over soon. He wished he were home, drinking beer, and feeling sorry for himself.

"Listen," Joseph went on. "Trust me, she's a very unhappy person."

Bob almost laughed out loud at that. "Yeah, she looks absolutely miserable," he said mockingly, cringing, as yet again the handsome stranger placed a soft kiss on Marlena's lips and she smiled up at him. He wanted to yell out that those lips belonged to him, and that this creep had no business making contact of any kind with them.

"Bob," Joseph said. "Look at me." Bob did as he was told, and looked Joseph deep in his coal black eyes.

"She is miserable, this schmuck is only gonna make her happy for so long, but within a year, if not sooner, she'll be miserable again. Marlena has an emptiness inside of her that only God can fill, she tries to fill it with things, thinking that new couch or that new dress, or that new haircut will make her happy. And those things do for a short while, but then on it's on to the next thing, or in this case her next relationship."

"Will she ever find that happiness she's looking for?" Bob asked, watching them dance.

"She will, but I'm afraid it won't be for a long time. She'll spend many lonely years searching for a way to fill that void. Someday she'll regret divorcing you, but that won't be for awhile."

"So, I guess that means we really are finished?" Bob asked sadly.

"Yes, but you are a mensch, Bob. You're gonna go on to find happiness. God has great things in store for you."

"Really?"

"Yes, really. Okay, it's time for us to go now." Joseph said extending his hand.

Bob took his hand, then quickly took it back. "How do you know all this Joseph? I mean you do spend most of your time as a little Nativity Set figure. How are you able to do all this?" he said pointing around. "Like bring me here to see Marlena."

Joseph didn't feel like explaining all of it. These goyim could be draining with all their questions, so he said the only thing he could think of to Bob, "It's none of your business, now take my hand. Carol will be home soon."

Bob laughed and didn't press it any further. He supposed he should just be happy knowing that Joseph said God had great things in store for him. Bob took Joeph's hand, closed his eyes, and when he opened them, he was back in Carol's living room. Joseph was little again and back at the manger.

"Thank you, Joseph" Bob called out to him. "You've done me a great favor."

"I know, I know. Oh, and by the way the stove is fine. I just needed an excuse to get you here. Now get your stuff together. Carol will literally be home any minute. You don't want her walking in, and wondering why you're in her living room, now do you?"

No, her certainly didn't. He ran out to the kitchen and collected all his tools. When he was satisfied that he had everything and that the stove was off, he waved to the little PJ and raced out the door, nearly knocking down Carol in his quest to not look like some kind of weirdo.

"I'm so sorry," he said, embarrassed.

Carol laughed. "It's okay. It's that time of year, we're all rushing here or there, aren't we? Just as I was leaving the store today, I was nearly taken out by a man who looked to be at least a hundred whose cart was filled with ice cream, Yodels, wrapping paper and Depends. I couldn't help but laugh to myself, thinking of the newspaper heading: - 'Store employee buried under mountain of Depends and wrapping paper, but manages to eat her way through the ice cream and Yodels, thereby saving her life.'

Bob laughed too, realizing for the first time how pretty and funny she was. Before he was too preoccupped by Marlena to notice any other females, but this one definitely had his attention now. And against his best intentions, he found himself drawn to her.

"Sorry," she laughed again, "I have a strange sense of humor."

"Don't be sorry, that was funny." Bob said, staring into her big green eyes.

"So, the stove's all set?" Carol asked.

"Yes, it is, are you having a lot of people over for Christmas dinner?"

"No, just me and Simon, but my eldest son, Jack and his girlfriend will be coming the next day, so I need to prepare something respectable for them," she answered, laughing again.

He had never met someone who laughed so much. He knew he should have just wished her a Merry Christmas and gotten into his truck to leave, but he couldn't, he was transfixed by her. It was like he was the moth and she was the flame, so he asked her more questions.

"Are you a good cook?"

"Depends on who you ask, but most sane people would disagree with that statement. I can make a decent ham, it's already cooked anyway, throw it in and walk away." She laughed.

"What about you? What are you doing for Christmas?"

He wasn't sure how to answer this, so he decided to be honest. "Nothing. My sister invited me to her house but I think I'm going to decline."

"How come?" Carol asked, suddenly serious.

"Because my wife left me a few months ago, and I can't go somewhere and fake Christmas cheer that I'm not feeling."

Carol could respect that and understand it as well. "I'm so sorry to hear that. I know how hard that can be, especially at Christmas, it feels like the whole world is celebrating except you. Last year my husband had left, and I was alone for Christmas, just me and my two sons. It was the toughest Christmas of my life. I just wanted to stay in bed all day but I couldn't; I had to make it as merry as I could especially for Simon, who had been through enough already. But it gets easier, one day you'll wake up and it won't hurt so much."

"Thank you, he said, and meant it. "And I'm sorry about all you've been through with your divorce and with your sons; I'm sure it's been a long and difficult road for you. You must be a strong woman, Carol."

Carol smiled again. "Well, I don't know about that, I was only strong because I had to be for my sons; it's amazing how much strength you can muster up when you love someone. If it had just been me, I might have curled up in a ball and stayed that way for awhile. But I had to think on my feet. I had been a housewife forever and then all of sudden I had to get a job, move out of my house, and put a good deal of my possessions in storage, which I ended up losing anyway because I couldn't pay my storage fee."

It was Bob's turn to smile. "Well, that sounds like a strong woman to me, when you can put aside you're own personal pain and heartache, and single handedly save your family; that sounds pretty heroic to me."

Carol had to laugh at that, nobody had ever called her heroic before, but she didn't mind it either. Before she could stop the words from coming out of her mouth she asked, "Why don't you come to our house for Christmas dinner? It won't be anything spectacular but I can throw something together, and they'll be no pressure on you to act festive. We can be miserable together."

Bob thought about it for only a moment, and then answered, "Sure, why not. What time?"

"How about around two?" She couldn't believe she had just asked Bob, who was virtually a stranger, for Christmas dinner, but this was different Carol; her experience with the Dime Store Joseph had changed her forever.

"Perfect," Bob said. "Should I bring anything?"

"Just your smile, oh, that's right," she paused, "we're having a smile-free Christmas."

Bob laughed, "I think I can manage to smile for a few hours on Christmas Day, but just a few." In fact, he knew he could, especially if Carol was around. He hated to admit it to himself but suddenly he was crushing on the pretty lady with the big green eyes.

"Okay, Bob, I've enjoyed our conversation, but I need to go in wrap the rest of Simon's presents before he gets home. It's so hard when he's home because he keeps pestering me, or accidently walking into my room if I forget to lock the door. Waiting isn't one of Simon's strong suits."

"It isn't one of mine either." Bob said jokingly, then added, "I've enjoyed talking with you as well, Carol. All right, I'll see you at two on Christmas Day."

"Sounds good," she said as she opened the door.

Bob walked toward his truck and called out, "Thank you, Carol."

She yelled back, "You're very welcome, Bob."

Both Bob and Carol couldn't help but smile for the rest of the day.


Christmas Time
   Ten Years Later...
   Beth


"Mom, it's me," Beth said gently as she walked into her mother's room at Baystate Extended Care Facility. Her mother stared at with a blank expression on her face. It broke Beth's heart to see her once beautiful mother looking so haggard and old. Her long silky chestnut hair, once a such a source of pride for her mother, was graying and unkempt, and shorter than Beth had ever seen it. Her mother's shapely figure was now skeletal and wrapped in a faded red bathrobe which was too large on her emaciated frame. Only the eyes were the same, still lovely, but still had the ability to bore holes in Beth's head.

"Merry Christmas," Beth said as she reached over to give her mother a hug. Her mother moved away so Beth couldn't reach her.

"Where's Linda?" her mother asked lifting up her head, which was usually slumped over as if it were too heavy to hold up.

"I don't know, she's not here though," Beth said, repeating her usual answer.

"Well, tell her I want to see her," her mother said angrily. "And she better not be with your father; I told her to stay from him."

Beth knew she had to change the subject, whenever her mother talked about Linda she got combative. It had taken Beth awhile to figure out who Linda was, but through talking to other family members she had learned that her father had left her mother for Linda, and although her mother couldn't remember much, she could sure remember Linda.

Thankfully her mother was easily distracted, so Beth said as cheerfully as she could, "Look, I brought you something," she said holding out a festively decorated package.

"What's this?" her mother asked, taking the gift from her.

"It's a Christmas present, silly. Now open it."

"What is it? A bomb, you're trying to kill me, aren't you?"

"No," Beth said laughing. She knew better than to be offended; she knew it was the disease. Not only did her mother not know who she was most of the time, but her mother was also paranoid, and thought everyone was out to get her.

"Trust me, just open it; you're going to love it."

Her mother carefully ripped open the paper, and threw it to Beth. "Save that paper now, it's expensive, you were always such a wasteful creature." Beth laughed to herself; her mother had called her many things over the years, but never a "creature."

She tore open the box to find a teddy bear wearing a white sweater with a Christmas tree and red ornaments on it. Her mother smiled lovingly at it.

"Squeeze it's tummy," Beth said excitedly. Her mother did and smiled as the bear played 'Jingle Bells.'

"Well, isn't that cute," her mother said hugging the bear to herself. The bear then played 'Silent Night.'

Just then one of her mother's care workers came in to check on her. Her mother, with all the enthusiasm of a child on Christmas morning, held up the bear, and said, "Look what my daughter, Beth, gave me for Christmas."

The worker came over to get a closer look and gush about how adorable it was. For Beth it was a big moment, first of all, it was one of the few times since her mother had come down with the disease that her mother had actually known Beth was her daughter. At times, she had lucid moments, and it appeared as though she knew Beth and remembered certain things about their relationship, but most times, she just referred to Beth as that nice girl who came to visit.

Second of all, it was the only other time she had liked Beth's Christmas gift to her. The first time was when Beth was sixteen and had given her mother that lovely hat and scarf set suggested by Maggie. Beth remembered that morning as if it had been yesterday, she remembered squirming nervously as her mother slowly opened her present. She remembered clearly also being prepared for a negitive reaction from her mother. But to her surprise, her mother smiled, as she carefully held up the delicate scarf, eyeing it, and then the hat.

"Why thank you," her mother had said, "it's beautiful." Beth had felt like she had solved world hunger or something; it was her best Christmas to date.

Within a few short years after that her mother had started to exhibit bizarre behavior. Beth recalled when she was twenty-two and her mother was fifty-six, which is a little young for the disease, and she had called her to wish her a Happy Easter, and her mother exploded on her, accusing her of releasing ants in her house becuase they were everywhere. At the time Beth didn't think much of it, she figured, it was just her mother being her mother. But as time went on, Beth knew it was much more than that, especially when her mother didn't seem to know who she was. "Beth who?" she'd ask when Beth called her. The final straw came when a neighbor phoned Beth and said, "Please come, your mother's outside throwing her dishes everywhere yelling, 'Wash yourself.' "

Beth went and so did the local sheriff, and it was determined that her mother needed a mental health evaluation. Her disease finally had a name, and it was Dementia; it was a cruel and merciless disease, one that made you grieve a living person as though they were dead. At that moment everything changed.

Her mother had to move into a full-time care facility and Beth had to get her mother's affair in order, a heavy demand for a young woman of only twenty-four.

It was then that words of the Dime Store Joseph came back to her, ever so clearly. Never would she have imagined that her mother, who seemed so powerful at times, would be rendered so powerless, so much so that she couldn't pick out her own clothes, barely knew what day it was, couldn't brush her teeth without supervision, but all those years ago, Joseph had told her to love, so she did.

And, then the moment Beth had been waiting for all her life arrived, her mother, out of the blue said to her caretaker, "Did I ever tell you about my daughter, Elizabeth? She was the cutest little girl, I called her Beth. She was born with these huge hazel eyes, and not a hair on her head, but she had this smile, I tell ya, she could have been a baby model. She's a good girl, a very good girl, and I'm so proud of her. I hope she comes to visit soon, I miss her terribly. I wasn't always the kindest mother, I want to see her and tell her I'm sorry, and that I love her."

Beth wanted to say, "I'm here, its me Beth." But instead she excused herself, as the tears coursed down her cheeks. "I'll be right back, Mom."

"Okay, Maria," her mother said. Beth had no idea who Maria was but it didn't matter, because she knew somewhere beyond Dementia, beyond pain, her mother loved her and was proud of her, and that was all she needed; it was truly her best Christmas ever.


Simon

Simon looked at all the gorgeous necklaces but none of them quite lived up to his mother. She had been his rock for so many years, and he wanted a gift which would reflect that, but really how could an object live up to the feelings in his heart? Something could cost a million dollars and wouldn't do justice to how he felt about his mother. She was there for him always, during his ups and his downs, and many times in the past he'd been angry at her, but as he got older he realized one thing- she was the one constant in his life. She loved him when he was unlovable, cheered for him when he was at the bottom, and gave him her smile when that's all she had to give. Crap, he felt frustrated, there had to be something, but maybe he should just find something and be satisfied with it. Love went so deep, how could any object come close to portraying it, and who could measure it, who could even try? He finally decided on a beautiful golden heart pendant necklace. He would pour all his love into that necklace, it would be enough; he knew his mom would love it.

He gladly paid the two hundred dollars for it, and walked the few blocks back to his dorm room at Framingham State to pack his things for Christmas break with the lovely necklace in his pocket. He passed a big Nativity Set outside of a catholic church, and as was his custom, he waved to the Joseph figure, this time he could have sworn Joseph winked at him. He knew, at that moment, this was going to be one of his best Christmases ever.


Bob and Carol


Bob smiled at his wife as they prepared their Christmas dinner together. Bob always prepped the turkey, while Carol handled the sides. Carol was excited for the day, Simon was there, home on Christmas break. Jack and his wife, Juliana, would be coming with their baby, a little angel named

Allegra, meaning happy; the perfect name for the perfect baby, Carol thought. Beth would be coming as well, they considered her family now, and they loved her as if she were their own daughter.

"Mommy, how do I look?" five-year-old Eva asked as she twirled around in her sparkly red Christmas dress.

"Why, you look like the most beautiful little princess I've ever seen," Carol gushed.

Eva blushed at the compliment from her mother and before she knew what was happening, she was being lifted in the air by her father.

"Yes, but she'll always be MY princess, remember you were daddy's princess first when all those boys start coming around."

"She's only five, Bob," Carol laughed. "I sincerely hope we have a few years before we have to worry about that."

"We better," he said planting kisses all over Eva's face.

"Daddy, put me down," she giggled, "I have stuff to do."

"Like what?" he asked, putting her down.

"Like making the Christmas placemats for everyone." That had been Eva's job since she was three years old, and one she took very seriously.

"Okay, kid, go make your placemats; your mother and I will finish slaving over our Christmas meal." The little girl ran away before anyone could stop her. Her parents smiled at each other, just as in love as when they had spent that first Christmas together ten years ago.

Eva had been an unexpected gift born to a heroin addicted mother and a father who had been in an out of jail. Nobody wanted her, as she was developmentally slow and not expected to reach appropriate developmental milestones. She was in foster care until she was six months old before Carol learned from a close friend that there was a little baby girl who needed a permanent home. It broke Carol's heart to hear that there was a little girl who was unwanted. She discussed it with Bob and all it took was one meeting with the tiny infant for them to seal the deal and decide to go forward with the adoption. By the time Eva was a year old, she was officially their daughter. Under the love and care of her new parents the child grew and developed, surpassing all expectations.

Life was good for Bob, the words of porcelain Joseph had truly come to fruition; life was better than he could have ever imagined it would be. First, meeting Carol after that strange afternoon spent with PJ showing him Marlena with her boy toy, then becoming a father to that sweet little girl. He never in his wildest dreams thought he'd become a father; it was more than he could fathom at times, and truly he felt unworthy. It made up for each and every tear he had ever shed over Marlena. Life was beautiful and Bob was grateful.

They continued preparing the meal together, Carol humming, thinking how blessed she was to have met someone like Bob. He was her very best friend, gentle and kind, and always making her laugh. They married within two years of meeting, and when they did Bob had said to her, "Let's pick out a house together. I want you to have your own house, not one filled with the ghost of Marlena, but a place to start our own memories together." They had picked out a charming restored Victorian with four bedrooms, and loads of character. Carol adored it, especially at Christmas time, when it looked like something out of a fairy tale. With all the lights and decorated trees, Bob would jokingly say he felt like he lived at the North Pole.

By two in the afternoon everyone was seated around the table, and Bob was preparing to say grace, when Eva got up and said, "Wait." Everyone looked around expectantly to see what would come next. Ten month old Allegra giggled her little baby giggle. Her mother shushed her, and her father smiled at her, his eyes just as big and blue as hers. After what seemed like forever, their food in front of them getting cold, Eva returned with the Dime Store Nativity Set and placed it in the middle of the table.

"They should be here with us too, after all, it is their day," she declared. Nobody could argue with that logic, so the Holy Family was set up in the middle of the table. Bob said grace, and Eva looked around while all the other members of her family had their heads bowed and eyes closed. She looked at the Holy Family and saw the little Joseph with his head bowed too. He lifted his head and made eye contact with Eva. He brought his finger to his lips to shush her. As soon as the prayer was over Joseph went back to standing beside Mary and looking just like any other porcelain figure. Eva knew Christmas was magical but she didn't know Nativity Set figures came to life. She kept the encounter to herself, figuring with her childlike innocence, anything was possible at Christmas time.

It would be years later when Eva was going through her own teenage angst that the Dime Store Joseph would appear to her... "Oy! You teenage girls are impossible..." He was heard saying.


Epilogue


Porcelain Joseph continued his ministry of helping goyim in need, whenever there was a goy in trouble, he was there. But truth be told he was looking forward to his retirement, if he had to listen to another goy ask, "WHY?" well, he might just explode...

# Also by Kathleen Kilgallon

**The Tommy and Kindra Series**
Planted

**Standalone**
The Dime Store Joseph

# About the Author

Kathleen Kilgallon loves nature, a good hike in the woods, a walk on the beach, and laughing with those she loves. She is the author of In Bloom, and it's long-awaited follow-up Planted.

Her newest book is The Dime Store Joseph a Christmas story filled with magic, wonder, and a Joseph figure who works his way into people's hearts and lives.

# About the Publisher